
Prince Charles

England's Future King

by Jean Nugent

DILLON PRESS, INC. MINNEAPOLIS, MINNESOTA

Library of Congress Cataloging in Publication Data

Nugent, Jean.
Prince Charles, England's future king.

(Taking part)
Summary: A biography of the heir to the thousand-year-old British throne.
1. Charles, Prince of Wales, 1948- —Juvenile literature. 2. Great Britain—Princes and princesses—Biography—Juvenile literature. [1. Charles, Prince of Wales, 1948- . 2. Princes] I. Title.
DA591.A33N83 941.085'092'4 [B] [92] 81-22183
ISBN 0-87518-226-7 AACR2

Second printing 1983

Dillon Press, Inc., 500 South Third Street
Minneapolis, Minnesota 55415

Printed in the United States of America

PRINCE CHARLES

His Name and Titles: Charles Philip Arthur George Mountbatten-Windsor; Prince of Wales; Duke of Cornwall; Duke of Rothesay; Earl of Carrick; Earl of Chester; Baron of Renfrew; Lord of the Isles; Great Steward of Scotland; Knight of the Most Noble Order of the Garter; Knight of the Most Ancient and Most Noble Order of the Thistle; Great Master and Principal Knight Grand Cross of the Most Honorable Order of Bath; and heir to the thousand-year-old British throne and one of the largest fortunes on earth, well over $140 million.

His Job: Apprentice King.

He Earns: $1 million yearly from the Duchy of Cornwall.

He Owns: Two large estates; one country home; two apartments; a dozen horses; a jeeplike vehicle; and a sports car.

He Uses: A fleet of Rolls-Royces and airplanes (with fighter escort); the royal train; and the royal yacht *Britannia.*

Yearly He: Skis in Switzerland; fishes in Iceland; summers in Scotland; and winters at Sandringham.

His Sports: Jogging; wind surfing; scuba diving; cross-country riding; water skiing; and wild boar hunting.

Interesting Facts about Him: Carries no money; instead, an aide pays for everything; hates his big ears and people who call him Charlie; likes music and practical jokes; collects cartoons.

Friends Say of Him: He spends much more time working at his desk than playing.

He Says of Himself: "I have not decided . . . what mark I would like to make on history. I . . . only hope it won't be a messy mark!"

Major Events in His Life

His Birth: November 14, 1948, in Buckingham Palace, London, England, to Princess (now Queen) Elizabeth and Prince Philip.

His Mother Is Crowned Queen of England: June 2, 1952.

He Becomes Prince of Wales: July 1, 1969.

His Marriage to Lady Diana Spencer: July 29, 1981.

A sleepy Prince Charles is held by his proud parents, Princess (now Queen) Elizabeth and Prince Philip.

Long ago, in a kingdom torn by war, good people—the king's people—waited outside tall palace gates. Rain drizzled through a thick fog, and hours passed. Still they waited, watching for a sign from inside the old palace called Buckingham.

Finally it came. Doors flew open, and yellow light pierced the fog. A white-stockinged footman sped to the gates, then whispered in a policeman's ear.

"It's a boy!" the policeman shouted. "England has a new prince!"

Whistles and cheers, laughter and clapping filled the night air. Bells rang out in celebration. The weary faces of Britons broke into smiles of hope. A new prince—a new era!

The British had just come through a terrible war with the Germans, and they had won that long, hard fight. Now Elizabeth, their princess, and her husband Philip had given them what they needed most—a royal promise that once again things would be as they had always been for England. Steady. Constant. With the House of Windsor leading them on.

Fame belonged to Prince Charles Philip Arthur George Mountbatten-Windsor from the second he was born on November 14, 1948. On that night behind palace walls, the new baby fell asleep to the sound of cheering crowds. Crowds and grand pageants would mark each crossroad in his life.

At first life for the young prince wasn't so different from the lives of many English children. Elizabeth and Philip wanted their son to grow up like other boys. Charles, however, could never really be just like other boys.

Like other children, he played with toys, and his room housed the usual toy guns, blocks and stuffed animals. But some things that he took for granted were amazing to most boys and girls.

At mealtimes Charles spread his rolls with butter slices shaped like the royal coat of arms. He wore wool coats stitched in the gold letters *H.H.* for "His Highness." He played with sheets of stamps showing rows of tiny Prince Charles pictures. And before his sister Anne was born in 1950, his playmates were adults—Nanny Lightbody who slept in his room, and Detective Kelley who shadowed Charles on his outings.

One more thing made him different from other children. His parents were gone much of the time. Prince Philip was a naval officer who came home only when he was on leave. Elizabeth's royal duties often took her away for months.

When the princess was asked if she and Philip missed the children during their travels, she said, "I'm afraid, more than they miss us." After all, the children were cared for by a doting grandmother. Most Britons knew her as the Queen Mother.

Whenever Elizabeth left London, Charles and

Anne were driven across the park to "Old Buck." That was the same drafty, 600-room palace in which Charles was born. Once there, Granny fussed and spoiled them. Then each night before bed they ran down dark palace halls to visit Grandpa England, known to the world as King George VI.

It was on one such visit that Charles found his life changed forever. In one moment he played with Anne and Nanny Lightbody. In the next Grandpa England was dead.

No longer could his mother spare even the few hours each day she spent with him when she was at home. No longer would familiar corners and closets of Clarence House be part of his days. From then on, Mummy was the queen of England.

Charles was suddenly the Duke of Cornwall, Duke of Rothesay, Earl of Carrick, Baron of Renfrew, Lord of the Isles, Great Steward of Scotland, and next in line to be king of England when his mother stepped down or died. That was a big job for a three-year-old!

Queen Elizabeth, Princess Anne, Prince Charles, and Prince Philip wave to a crowd from the balcony of Buckingham Palace.

Still puzzled by the royal court life going on around him, Charles was thrust into it all at once. Never again would he have as much freedom to do as he pleased.

For the most part Charles and Anne were well-behaved. Now that their mother was the queen of England, however, news reporters watched them constantly. The reporters looked, it seemed, for anything the children did wrong. Then they wrote stories about Charles and Anne which were read by millions of people.

What the reporters saw was a brother and sister who were opposites. Charles, quiet and shy, was fearful of the attention given to him. Still, he did enjoy his role as the watchful protector of little Anne. Unlike Charles, the tiny princess was a mischief maker. She was outgoing, sassy, and much more likely to give the writers something to report.

When the children were asked to watch their steps, Charles watched Anne's step more than his own. Palace visitors chuckled at the way Charles corrected his small sister.

"Don't laugh at the ladies' hats, Anne," said Charles. "No matter how funny they are!"

Another time Charles told her, "Don't stick your tongue out at the nice people. They've come to see you!" Charles warned Anne about this rule because he knew what would happen if she didn't obey. When Charles had broken the rule, he had earned himself a well-placed swat on the bottom.

Because Anne looked up to her big brother, she went along with him most of the time. Once in a

Anne, 3, and Charles, 5, pose together for a picture.

while, though, she thought of something else to try. Charles still remembers the game that Anne made up soon after they moved into Buckingham Palace.

Even before the family had settled into their new quarters, the children began exploring the endless maze of palace hallways. As they skipped past one, two, three palace guards, the guards had to clank swords, stamp boots, and slap caps in a salute to royal family members. Anne found that she could make the noises go on and on by walking back and forth in front of them. Imagine the poor tired guards. And imagine poor Charles who kept trying to tell Anne that playing with the guards wasn't the proper thing to do.

Anne wasn't the only one who needed correcting. Nanny, Papa, or Mummy scolded Charles sometimes when he played pranks of his own. Please don't put half-eaten candies in Granny's gloves, Charles. And never, ever again put ice down the footman's neck! Remember, your mother will soon be crowned queen of England.

People rushed here and there as Elizabeth's coronation, or crowning ceremony, neared. On the special day, Mummy, Papa, and Granny were tearful—happy tears, they told Charles. For Charles the best part of that day was wearing good-smelling hair stuff and leaving Anne at home while he watched from Westminster Abbey.

For his mother, the coronation was the start of work—always work! One afternoon a few weeks later, Charles and Anne slipped downstairs to their mother's office. Seeing her surrounded by papers, they asked if she would come and play.

The new queen of England looked up. "If only I could," she sighed.

In a few more years, Charles would see the magical coronation for what it really was—a crossroad in his life. Suddenly his family had important new duties to carry out. Although his mother carried out these duties cheerfully, they weren't always welcome to her. They weren't always welcome to Charles and Anne, either.

One of the harshest duties asked of Charles

was leaving home when he was eight years old. Early in 1953, Philip and Elizabeth decided that Charles should be educated in a boarding school away from home. He would be the first future king of England to have this kind of schooling.

His parents had good reasons for sending their son away to school. Charles was held apart from people. For him to be a wise and respected king, he needed to know a world wider than the grounds of "Old Buck." In the fall of 1957, he was driven 56 miles from home and dropped off at Cheam, Prince Philip's old boarding school.

Charles remembers that day as one of the worst in his life. In just 24 hours, he went from the richness of Buckingham Palace to a bleak, unheated room. Even worse, he had to share it with strangers. Charles was expected to clean his room, wait on tables, stand in line for baths twice a week, and put up with his classmates' insults. This new kid—number 89—was keenly aware of being alone and being different.

On the rugby field Charles startled other

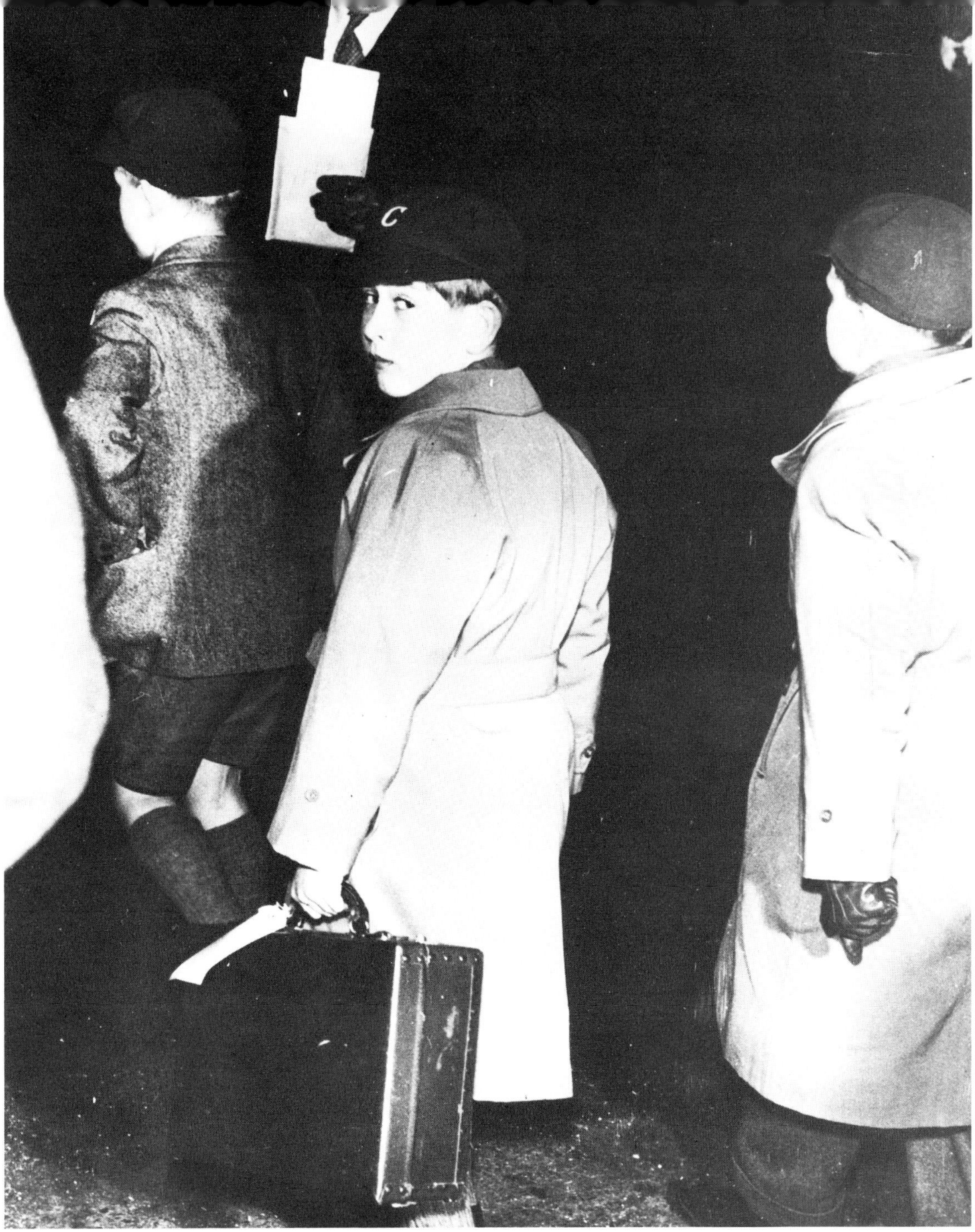

Charles wasn't very happy about leaving home to go to school at Cheam.

players by saying, "I'm sorry" to everyone he tackled. In Sunday chapel, he was uneasy when prayers for the royal family were said. Once he muttered, "I wish they prayed for the other boys, too."

A few months after Charles started school, his mother announced that she was making him Prince of Wales. "I intend to create my son Charles Prince of Wales today. When he is grown up, I will present him to you at Caernarfon."

Eleven years later that "presenting" ceremony, called an investiture, would take place at the ancient Welsh castle. At that time Charles would begin to carry out the duties that went with this princely title.

Charles was also named Earl of Chester and Knight Companion of the Most Noble Order of the Garter. All of his new titles were cheered by his classmates at Cheam. Titles, however, did not help Charles make friends at school. Instead, newspaper reporters did that by printing a false story.

One reporter discovered that Charles didn't get much spending money at school. The reporter wrote a newspaper story about the "poor" little prince. In it he said Charles was kept so poor by penny-pinching parents that he sold his clothes for "sweets" money.

When the story appeared in the United States, America's candymakers were shocked. Right away a group of them mailed a goodwill package to Charles. It held everything that a youngster might want—bubble gum, jelly beans, peanut butter, and Tootsie Rolls.

Wide-eyed, Charles listened as the Cheam headmaster read a note tacked to the crate. "We were told the prince was short of candy, so our committee [decided] to. . .help him out of a jam."

Another of Charles's favorite memories from Cheam was his part in one of the yearly school plays. In a 1960 play called *The Last Baron*, Charles had an important job. He was to learn the star's lines and actions, and then stand back and wait. Charles was the understudy. That meant he would go on stage only if the leading actor could not perform.

One night the star was sick, and Charles the understudy became Prince Charles the star. People in the audience that night were pleased to see the young prince on stage. They wondered, though, why Queen Elizabeth and Prince Philip weren't there to share their son's success. Soon a message arrived for Charles that explained everything. His mother had just given birth to a baby boy named Andrew.

Now Prince Charles had his own understudy. If something unexpected ever happened to him, tiny Prince Andrew would take his place as the next king of England.

During his five years at Cheam, Charles was known as a fair student who kept to himself. A friend remembers that Charles was deeply hurt when he had to leave his home and family. That homesick feeling would trouble him for years to come.

Still, as difficult as Cheam had been, Charles's

next school in Scotland was worse. Gordonstoun, with its cold showers and long morning runs, was a bit frightening for any 13-year-old.

Pit them against nature. It breeds tough men. That was the school's idea. Firefighting, mountain rescues, and ocean life-saving were a part of every-day life for the boys of Gordonstoun.

Soon after he came to the Scottish school, Charles spent a weekend with his grandmother. He appealed to her. Get me out of this place! She listened but said no. Charles must be strong

While a student at Gordonstoun, Charles learned to play polo.

and stay at Gordonstoun. Firmly, lovingly, his grandmother, mother, and father were preparing him to be King Charles III.

Later, when his socks and shirts were taken for souvenirs, and his notebooks were stolen and sold to a foreign newspaper, he did not get upset. Charles was accepting his special place in the world.

When Charles was 15, he made a quick trip home from Gordonstoun to meet another newborn brother, Prince Edward. Charles laughed and played with Edward and enjoyed the happy times with his family. Besides, time at home meant less time at school!

Charles had almost finished his studies at Gordonstoun when a chance came for him to go to school far away from Scotland. The Australians invited him to attend a school in their country. Australia was halfway around the world and "down under" in the southern part of the earth.

Partly to satisfy the Australians, and partly to

give Charles a break, Elizabeth and Philip enrolled Charles at Timbertop. Timbertop was a country school not far from the Australian city of Melbourne.

For the first time in years Charles was free—free from the press, free from detectives at his heels, and free to roam, fish, or climb mountains as he wished. The seven months at Timbertop changed him from a shy young man to a friendly future king of England. Thanks to the fresh air, the freedom, and the kind Australians, Charles gained confidence in himself. He called Timbertop "the most wonderful experience [of my life]."

Other changes took place, too, as Charles turned 18 and started his studies at Trinity College in England. He became Councillor of State, Queen Elizabeth's advisor. Now, if something happened to his mother, he would become king of England. Before he was 18, a guardian would have been named to make decisions for him.

Elizabeth introduced Charles to "the boxes."

Dressed in his student robes, Charles is ready to begin his first day of classes at Trinity College.

These were worn cases which held papers that had to be read and signed by her each day. When Charles becomes king, he will be in charge of the boxes.

As Charles grew up, he became more and more a public figure. The English people liked him and wanted to know about his life. Since he was a member of the royal family, however, he did not have much time to himself. Sometimes it seemed that everything he did or said was reported in the newspapers.

For years the press had made up lists of "suitable brides" for Charles. Since he was old enough to date now, reporters wanted to know all about the young women he met. They demanded to know the *who*, *what*, and *where* of each meeting. If Charles didn't give them the answer they wanted to hear, they might make one up to fit their story.

For a long time Charles didn't enjoy dating because of the false stories written about him. "I've only. . .to look twice at someone, and next morning [the press has me] engaged to her!" he complained.

One "suitable bride" the press missed was the girl who played with Charles's younger brothers, Andrew and Edward. Charles didn't see eight-year-old Diana Spencer as a possible wife then, either. Hardly grown up himself, the prince often ignored Diana. Still, he cared enough to give her a children's book he had written. Afterward Diana remembered the book clearly. Charles hardly remembered it at all.

At the time other events were more important to the prince than young Diana. Charles was nearly 21, and his mother had made a promise to the people of Wales years before. "When he is grown up, I will present him to you at Caernarfon."

During the upcoming presenting ceremony—Charles's investiture as the Prince of Wales—he would greet the Welsh people for the first time. It might have been a happy time for him. But it wasn't.

Prince Charles dances with his cousin, 8-year-old Lady Sarah Armstrong-Jones. Charles gave a book to Diana Spencer when she was the same age.

The world had changed since Queen Elizabeth had promised to make Charles Prince of Wales ten years before. Now it was 1968, and many young people were against things old and costly. The investiture was both, and something more. For many young Welsh, it was also a matter of pride in their homeland. Wales had fallen to English armies seven hundred years before.

"Why should Wales celebrate its takeover by England," Welsh youth asked. "Why spend a million dollars on a pageant when we're out of work and hungry," other young protestors wanted to know.

Bombings and angry marches marked the year before the investiture. In spite of the anger, most older Welsh people wanted the ceremony. For them it was as if they were acting out their past. Having a Prince of Wales had been a part of their way of life for as long as they could remember.

Meanwhile, steps were taken by the royal family to ease bad feelings. Quietly, Charles began a crash course to learn the Welsh language and way of life. Throughout his stay at the United College of Wales, he studied language by day and met protestors by night. Little by little, he earned their respect.

Two months later, when Charles spoke to the protestors in perfect Welsh, they cheered him. Before long even some youthful Welsh warned,

"If anybody lays a finger on that lad, they'll swing from the nearest tree."

At last the day came for the investiture—July 1, 1969. Polished coaches rumbled through Welsh streets on their way to Caernarfon Castle. All around flags waved for the young prince. Royal jewels gleamed in the sunlight. Spirited horses pranced in line. Imagine a scene long ago from King Arthur's court, with Charles in the starring role. That was July 1, 1969, at Caernarfon.

At the ceremony Charles knelt before his mother. Choked with tears, he said the oath. "I, Charles, Prince of Wales, do become your liege man of life and limb and of earthly worship, and faith and truth. I will bear unto you to live and die against all manner of folks."

When he stood, he had taken on a lifetime job as the royal ruler and protector of Wales. He had also made a pledge to the Welsh people—*Ich Dien* ("I serve"). Charles took those words to be an order from God.

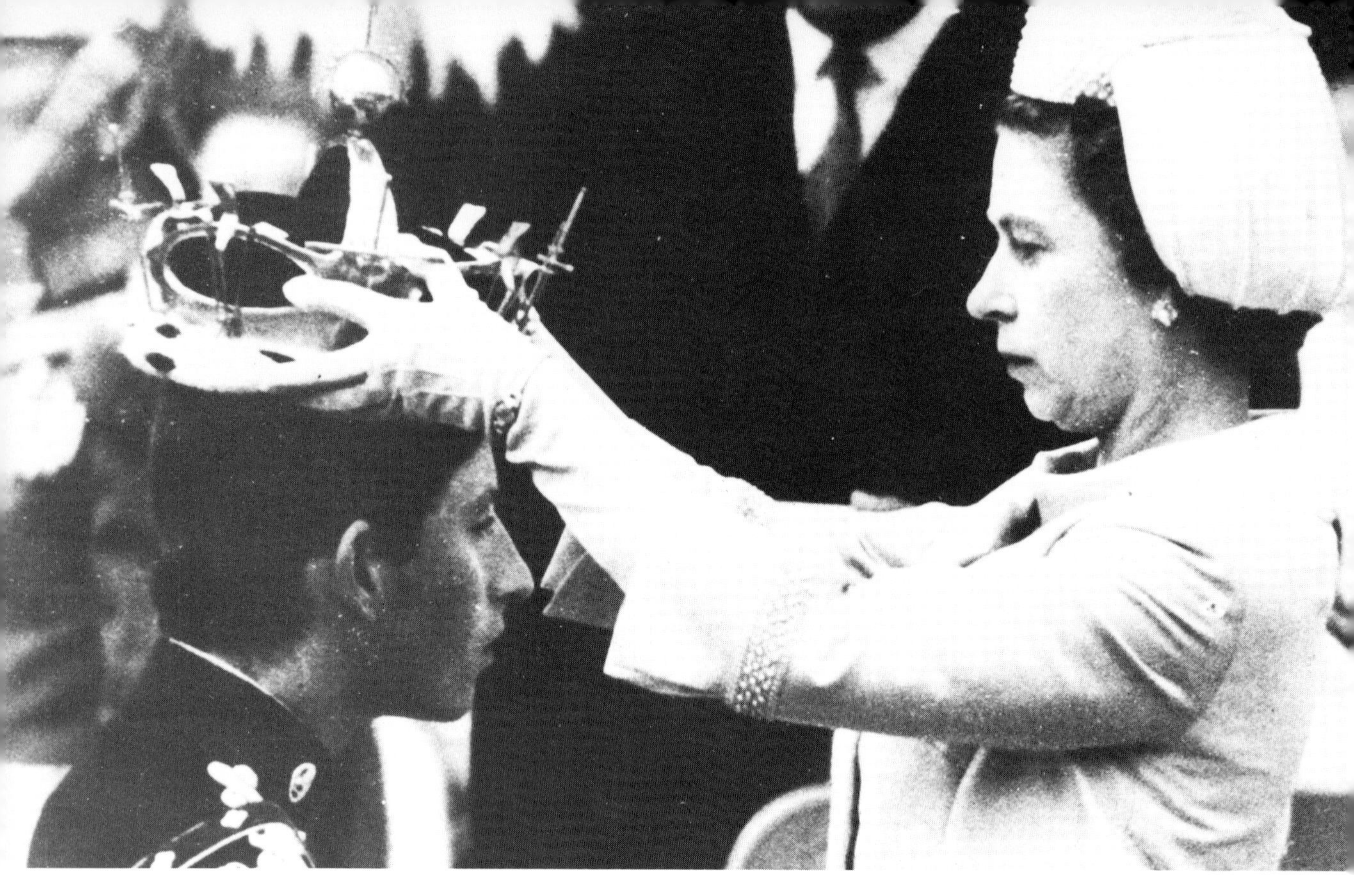

Queen Elizabeth crowns Charles the new Prince of Wales.

A year later Charles had finished college and was serving his country full time. As the Prince of Wales, he traveled to Japan, France, Mexico, and many other countries. Everywhere he went, he tried to help others understand the British people and their problems. One of the problems he talked about was lack of jobs. In fact, he turned his first official visit overseas into a job-hunting mission for Wales.

While touring the Japanese World's Fair, called Expo '70, Charles met the president of the Sony company. The president said that he wanted to build a new Sony plant in Western Europe. At once Charles suggested, "Why not try Wales?" Before long Charles persuaded the president that building the plant in Wales was a good idea. Two years later the prince cut the ribbon on Sony's new plant in Glamorgan, Wales. That Japanese trip meant steady jobs for several thousand Welsh workers.

Between trips around the world, Charles raised money for needy people in Great Britain. In 1970 he became a member of the House of Lords, the upper house of the British Parliament. Parliament makes the laws of Great Britain. Charles talked to members of Parliament about his special interests—helping young people find jobs, and settling racial problems.

For the Britons who watched him daily, the Prince of Wales was a pride and a pleasure. "What's he up to now?" many asked as they opened their newspapers. That was a good question because Charles was testing himself in new ways.

One of these new ways was serving in the British armed forces. Charles tried every daring job the army, air force, and navy could find.

In the air force the prince earned his flight wings along with other new cadets. He learned to pilot jet fighters, carrier planes, and helicopters. He also earned a special award for work with the Red Dragon Squadron of commando-helicopter pilots. Charles's air force flight instructors said he was a natural pilot. His fellow air cadets said he was a natural joker.

Of all the tricks he pulled, they remember his April Fool's joke the best. Charles asked the cadet caretaker to send out this notice: "All regular issue officers' shoes must be turned in at once. The maker has recalled them due to faulty heels." Many puzzled officers went shoeless for a day before sharing an "April Fool's, lads," with Prince Charles.

Prince Charles prepares to board a plane for his first parachute jump.

In the army the prince earned his paratroop jumping wings by parachuting from a plane. His paratroop commander, however, said he was *not* a natural paratrooper!

Charles remembers what happened when he jumped out of the moving plane. "Out I went. . . .I appeared to be flipped on [my] back and the next thing I knew my feet were above my head caught in the [chute] rigging lines. . . .I thought, they didn't tell me anything about this."

Charles's parachute had opened safely. Since his feet were tangled in the chute lines, though, he hit the water upside down. In ten seconds British marines pulled him from the water, safe and sound.

During the six years Charles spent in the armed forces, he served the longest time in the navy. Charles was stationed on four different ships. On the last ship, the minesweeper HMS *Bronington*, he was the skipper.

The most exciting thing Charles did in the navy was training as a frogman. Once, in the freezing waters of the far north, he dived under Arctic Circle ice. Dressed in his special cold water diving suit, the prince looked like a big balloon.

For Charles the best part of military service wasn't his daring deeds. Instead, his favorite time was spent on ships at sea. Those months away gave him the same freedom from the press he had known at Timbertop. That freedom, however, may have caused at least one unprincely meeting with reporters.

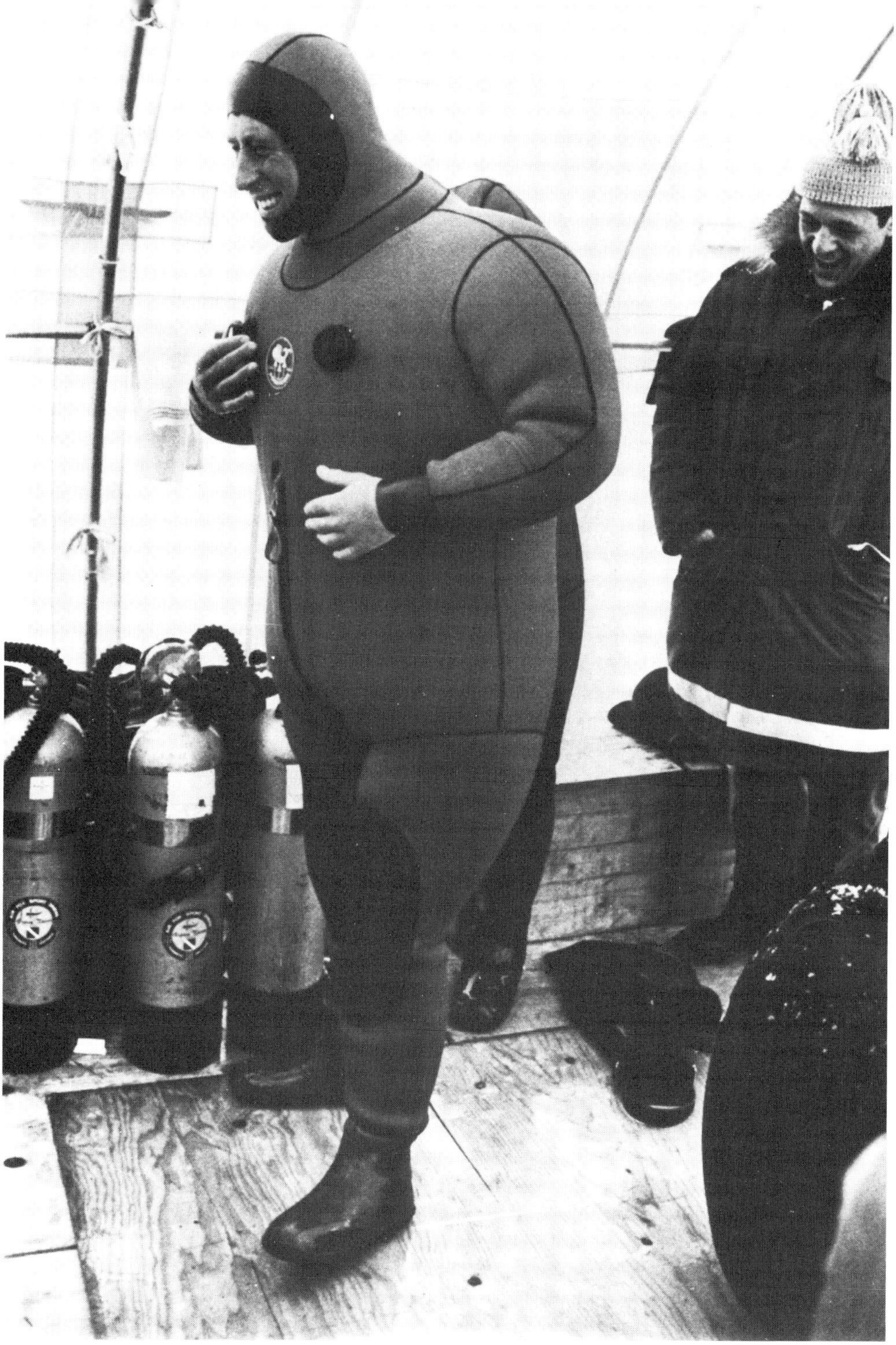

Dressed in his cold water diving suit, Charles looks like a big balloon.

While the HMS *Jupiter* was docked at a port in the United States, Charles heard some bad news. A masked gunman had tried to kidnap his sister Anne and her husband, Captain Mark Phillips. Anne's car was forced off the road by the gunman. A fight followed, and shots were fired. Although Anne and Mark were not harmed, their chauffeur, a guard, and a policeman were wounded before the gunman was stopped.

Charles was angry. Fearing for the safety of Anne and his whole family, he retreated to the ship to be alone with his thoughts. In minutes a noisy group of American newspaper reporters crowded onto the pier. Unknown to them, though, Charles had grown a beard at sea. When they reached the docked ship, all they saw was a scruffy, bearded man leaning over the railing.

"Hey, sailor," one of them yelled. "Get Prince Charles. We want to talk about the kidnapping."

"Oh, he won't see you," the sailor yelled back. "He's a . . . nasty piece of work!"

After a few minutes, the reporters left. They

didn't know the sailor was Charles, feeling too nasty to talk.

The fast-moving prince became an expert at throwing newspeople off his tracks. Charles was nicknamed "Royal Action Man" by reporters who couldn't keep up with him anymore. They couldn't keep up with his girlfriends, either, but they tried.

Charles enjoyed the company of beautiful women all over the world. "Charlie's Angels," the press called them. Sometimes the prince played a game of hide and seek meant to keep the press guessing. Two of his tricks were meeting at friends' homes and arriving places in different cars. Later, when the right young woman came along, these tricks would be put to good use.

Charles met Diana Spencer, now 16, in a field on her father's estate. Diana's sister had invited the 28-year-old prince to go on a pheasant hunt.

Diana and Charles laughed together and then went their own ways. Though Diana had admired the prince for years, she hid her feelings. Charles remembers thinking of Diana as "fun." At this time, though, he did not think of her as a marriage partner. After all, she was much too young for him, wasn't she?

Three years later, when Diana was 19, he decided to find out. By that time she shared an apartment with friends in London and worked at a kindergarten. Late one September night, a roommate handed Diana the phone.

"It's some man who says he's from Buckingham Palace. . . .It must be a joke!" she exclaimed. Diana giggled. She knew the caller was none other than Prince Charles.

Two months before, Aunt Lillibet (Queen Elizabeth) had asked Diana to join the royal family at Balmoral Castle. That was not unusual. Diana had been close to the family since she and the youngest princes, Andrew and Edward, had played together as children.

One thing did seem unusual, though. Every so often she caught Prince Charles watching her. Afterward, on board the royal yacht *Britannia*,

Prince Charles kept "happening by" to ask Lady Diana Spencer to walk with him.

Charles kept "happening by" when no one else was around. And Charles, along with Andrew and their friends, seemed to be hiding her from reporters.

One afternoon aboard the *Britannia*, Prince Andrew and another young couple leaped into small boats and raced off to different points in the bay. The press corps took up the chase, trying to get within camera range of the young people. As soon as the water chase started, Charles happened by again. This time he asked Diana to walk the decks with him.

Reporters never knew that Diana had been aboard the yacht. She didn't know what to think, either—until the phone rang that September.

After Charles's call Diana was asked to come again to Balmoral Castle. This time she knew the prince had asked her to come. Secretly, Diana was whisked off to the Queen Mother's home at Balmoral.

The couple met often after that. Happily, they found shared interests such as skiing, music, and walking together outdoors. Before long an ever watchful press began asking if Diana wasn't more than just another date.

"You mustn't rush me," Charles told them. But it was clear he had marriage on his mind.

"My marriage has to be forever, so I've got to choose carefully. . . .She marries into a way of life. . .a job,. . .in which she's got a contribution to make." He added quietly, "I hope I'm as lucky as my parents."

A few months later Charles told his parents of his feelings for Diana. Elizabeth and Philip approved the match. British officials gave their approval, too: the Privy Council, both Houses of Parliament, and judges ruling on the Royal Marriages Act of 1772. They had to approve because Charles was doing more than choosing a wife. He was choosing the next queen of England, too. She must be a very special person!

When the engagement was announced in February 1981, all agreed that Lady Diana Spencer of Althorp Manor was that very special person.

Quickly a golden net closed in on Diana. Just before the engagement became public, she moved into Clarence House. There Charles's grandmother, the Queen Mother, began teaching Diana how to be a public person. The royal family was helping her change from her old life into theirs.

While Diana followed the rules, she remained true to herself. She would stay Diana, even if "Her Royal Highness" was added to her name.

Charles and Diana after their engagement was announced.

No one was surprised when the young woman joined the Queen Mother for breakfast in blue jeans and a sweater. This soon-to-be Princess of Wales would set her own style!

Day by day, Lady Diana became the most watched woman in the world. She was acting out a real-life fairy tale with a storybook wedding.

"Isn't it wonderful!" older Britons exclaimed. Young people agreed, "He's picked a good one."

All over London, people rushed about preparing for the royal wedding. Special choirs and music groups practiced nightly for their parts in the ceremony. Teams of cleaning women, called "Mrs. Mops," polished Saint Paul's Cathedral until the huge church shone. Florists turned out hundreds of special street bouquets to decorate the wedding procession route. Bakers jammed their ovens with fruity cakes and sweets for the palace wedding parties.

At Buckingham Palace a government official took a stopwatch in one hand and notebook in the other. Then he mapped out every step of the royal wedding. He knew exactly what each person must do and how long that person should take to do it. No detail was left to chance.

Out in the English countryside, other experts were doing their part, too. At Worldwide Butterflies Limited, silkworms dined royally on leaves, and then spun and spun threads of silk for Diana's wedding gown. Boots and brass ornaments were polished. Everywhere, pictures of Lady Diana and Prince Charles were hung with brightly-colored banners. Britain was celebrating again.

On the wedding eve, fireworks lit the London sky. Pictures from Charles's life—his badges, crests, and awards—were sketched in fire sprays. At the finish a picture of Lady Diana with the prince filled the sky in dazzling bursts of color.

By the dawn of July 29, the streets were lined with thousands of people. At exactly 10 A.M. guards in bearskin hats arrived. One by one, they took their places along the route that the royal family would take to the wedding. Behind the guards horses from the queen's escort stepped high. Sparks flew from their hooves. On their backs red-coated palace guards sat stiff and straight.

First one royal coach, and then a second and a third, passed by the cheering crowds on the way to the wedding. Queen Elizabeth, Prince Philip, Anne, Edward, Andrew, and Charles arrived at Saint Paul's Cathedral. Finally, the bride's coach appeared. Diana, with her face hidden by a veil, waved to the crowds. Minutes later, she stepped onto the cathedral steps in a cloud of white silk and lace.

Inside the excited guests whispered, "The bride is here!" The swelling sounds of organ music filled Saint Paul's. Slowly, Diana and her father walked down the aisle to meet Charles.

To the outside world the wedding was a grand pageant of beautiful sights and sounds. The really important part, however, was taking place by the altar of the cathedral. There a young man and woman were making promises to be kept for life. After Charles and Diana said "I will," there were more words and the flash of a gold ring. Charles slipped the wedding band on Diana's waiting finger.

It was done. Private smiles passed between the Prince and the new Princess of Wales. They knew, though, that the world was still watching them. As they walked toward the crowds outside, Charles must have felt many things. Once more a grand pageant had changed his life.

As a young boy, he had watched his mother's coronation and had become England's future king. Later, he had knelt at the investiture at Caernarfon and had risen as the Prince of Wales. Now he was a husband. Holding Diana's hand, he knew that a final pageant remained—his own coronation, when he would be crowned King Charles III.

Right now that day is still a long way off. The Prince and Princess of Wales will have plenty of time—time to raise a family, and time to live out

Outside the bride and groom walk down the cathedral steps.

a lifetime of adventure. The family has already begun with the birth of their first child. The adventure will go on and on. For Charles and Diana are both very sure that their real-life fairy tale will end happily ever after.

The photographs are reproduced through the courtesy of Wide World Photos.

The Author

As an experienced free-lance writer, editor, publisher, and communications specialist, Jean Nugent has specialized in educational materials and fiction for young people. Her original radio drama series was broadcast on National Public Radio in 1981, and she created and wrote a recently released children's creative writing series.

This biography of Prince Charles, Ms. Nugent says, "gives readers a child's view of Charles's growing-up years, following him as he develops into a man with a whacky sense of humor and a keen sense of integrity." The author would like "to help young people understand that even larger-than-life characters from history books and today's newspapers are first people who share human feelings and problems with all of us."

Ms. Nugent attended Sacramento City College, Sacramento State College, and the University of California at Davis. She lives with her husband and two children in El Dorado Hills, California.